HOW TO RAISE CHICKENS:
From Baby Chicks To Egg-Laying Hens To Fryers

by Kjasen

Contents for Sections

Introduction

It's not hard to get wrapped up in the current popular craze of keeping backyard chickens. It seems like everyone you know has a couple of hens and a mini chicken coop in their back yard. And why not? There are many benefits to raising chickens. Some people do it for the sheer entertainment value that chickens provide. There is something relaxing and restorative about sitting on the back deck and watching chickens do what they do best. They are ridiculously amusing as they scratch around for a prize worm or insect and cluck proudly with puffed out feathered chest as though they own the world. There are also the chicken shenanigans. The great thing about the shenanigans is that you never know what the chickens will do or when they will do it. It's like a spontaneous surprise! This lends an element of excitement to keeping chickens.

Besides the entertainment value, the funny fowl give you the sense of slowing down and paying attention to something as simple as silly hens. You're reminded of simpler times when people, perhaps your grandparents or great-grandparents, actually had time to sit on the porch and admire their fine flock that provided them with fresh eggs and meat for Sunday dinner. In the complicated, fast-paced world in which most people live today, the sense of simpler times is welcomed.

But perhaps the most important reason that so many people are keeping backyard chickens is because of their desire for free-range, organic eggs and clean meat that does not contain antibiotics and is not from diseased chickens that have endured filthy and inhumane conditions before ending up at the supermarket. If you're one of the thousands upon thousands who have said *enough is enough* about the condition of store-bought meat and eggs, this guide, *How to Raise Chickens: From Baby Chicks To Egg-Laying Hens To Fryers* will prepare you to take the matter into your own hands and raise your own chickens. When you raise your own chickens, you know where the chickens came from, what they have eaten, and how they have been cared for. You determine the quality of the eggs and meat! You can eat fresh eggs and clean meat with a clear conscience and without fearing you are filling your body with unwanted harmful substances.

At first, you may feel a bit of intimidation about taking on the responsibility of chickens, but you'll gain confidence when you read this book and see that it's not that complicated to prepare for and keep a healthy flock of chickens. First, there are details that you need to know so you don't make costly mistakes. That's what this guide is all about. Read through it once, but keep it handy as a reference for checking the details as you go. Don't let it scare you away from the joy of owning your own flock of chickens.

Here's to a healthy and happy flock!

Section 1: The Legal Side of Raising Chickens

Anytime a person does something that could possibly affect others, there are usually legalities to consider. It is no different with raising chickens. Unless you live on land that is already specifically zoned for keeping farm animals, you may have a little homework to do before you can bring your flock home.

If you rent the property you live on, contact the property owner and ask

Ferhaterdem

about the farm animal policy for their rental property. If they permit chickens on the property, ask them for permission and any stipulations in writing to avoid any misunderstandings that could arise at a later date.

Getting permission from the property owner is just the first step. Whether you own or rent your property, if the property is governed by a homeowner's or neighborhood association, you will need to know and follow the association guidelines/rules. Often, the guidelines of these associations can be stricter than city guidelines. Even if the city permits chickens, your governing association may not allow it. Furthermore, these associations often have strict rules about the type of chicken coop you can build, including what color of paint may be used, size, and where it can be placed on the property.

You may also need clearance from the city and county in which you live. Some city ordinances and county zoning laws restrict the keeping of all or specific farm animals in the city limits, in certain areas of the city, or within a certain number of miles from the city. In some cases, chickens may be allowed but roosters are prohibited because of their early morning crowing habits. (Note that, unless you are trying to fertilize eggs, hens can survive just fine without a rooster to rule.) In many cases, there may be a limit to the number of hens one may keep. The general number of chickens allowed is usually from three to ten hens.

Additionally, there may be restrictions on the type of chicken coop that can be used, and there may be building permits required if you decide to build a large or multi-room chicken coop. Be sure you access city building codes for this information before you start planning your coop. In some areas, such as resort towns, getting permits for any type of building can be difficult and expensive.

Your city code regarding farm animals can often be found on the city's website. If not, try typing your city name and the words "municipal code" in your browser. The results should provide you with the information you need. If all else fails, call your city hall and ask how you can access the guidelines and laws regarding keeping poultry on your property.

Some city ordinances regarding chickens are very specific. The ordinances specify how many chickens may be kept, how large the coop may be, how far from the neighbors' fence or property the chickens and their coop must be kept, how often the coop must be cleaned, whether the chickens can run free on the property, and so forth.

Other city ordinances are vague and imply that if the chicken owners are responsible for the chickens, exercise common courtesy in not allowing the chickens to affect neighbors in a negative way, and do not create any safety, health, or sanitary issues, the chickens are permitted.

All across America, in cities and towns where chickens were prohibited before, people are fighting for the right to own and keep chickens in their backyard. Major cities such as Portland and Seattle are adopting chicken-friendly ordinances. If your city doesn't allow chickens, consider banding together with others and write letters petitioning your city council members to take action on behalf of those who want to raise chickens.

After you have become informed on the legal aspects of keeping chickens, you may want to visit with your immediate neighbors and get their feedback on your plan to get chickens. You don't have to get your neighbors' permission to raise chickens, but neighbors who do not want chickens in the neighborhood for any given reason can cause big trouble for the chicken owner. If this is going to be the case for you, it's best to know ahead of time so you can try to reason with the neighbor to avoid any future problems.

Even if you don't have a hesitant neighbor, it's a good idea to let all of your neighbors know of your plan for keeping chickens and to ensure them that your chickens won't disturb them or cause them any problems. You should inform them that you will keep the coop sanitary and clean, keep your chickens on your property, and will not tolerate a rooster that crows too early or too often. Give them your phone number and ask them to call you first if they ever have a complaint about your chickens instead of calling the city or the police. Assure them that you will take care of any issues immediately.

While chatting about your chickens, ask for your neighbors' cooperation in keeping their dogs and cats from roaming onto your property and upsetting your flock or worse.

Of course, you may be able to win your neighbors over to the side of the chickens if you extend a peace offering of fresh eggs or baked goods made with the fresh eggs.

Section 2: Choose Your Flock

Know the Purpose for Your Chickens

If you're reading this guide, you have probably put a lot of thought into keeping chickens and you probably have a purpose in mind for your chickens. Do you want chickens as pets? Plenty of people keep a couple of hens or a small flock for their entertainment value. Some claim that chickens can be trained to follow their owners, come to their owners when called, and cuddle like a cat or dog. At some pet or farm stores, you can find chicken treats, toys, and even diapers for hens that roam free in the house or take rides in the car.

Do you want to raise chickens to exhibit and compete in shows? There are several organizations and clubs that cater to those with show chickens, including the 4-H programs that can be found in most rural areas throughout the United States. For more information on how to choose show chickens, visit Poultry Show Central: http://www.poultryshowcentral.com/Breeder_Directory.html

Are rich, fresh eggs your goal? Do you want clean, organic meat? Certainly, chickens can provide this food for your family and maybe even extra to share. Many who raise chickens keep a large flock and sell eggs to their neighbors or at the farmers' market to earn back the money they invest in their chickens, and maybe more.

Knowing the specific purpose for your chickens can be helpful in choosing the chickens that are best suited for you.

Basic Chicken Terms

Before you choose your chickens, it can be helpful to know the terms that apply to chickens. Knowing the terms can be beneficial when ordering or buying chickens or talking about chickens with your fellow chicken owners. (Yes, there are thousands of them and you will most likely come across some!)

Chicken is a general term that applies to domesticated fowl. You may have also heard chickens referred to as chicks, hens, cocks, pullets, and cockerels. There are specific names that denote a chicken's gender and age. A **chick** is a baby chicken and remains so until the feathers come in. A **cockerel** is a male chicken that is less than one-year-old. A **pullet** is a female chicken that is less than one-year-old but is no longer a chick. An adult female chicken that has had its first molt, or feather shedding, is referred to as a **hen**. An adult male chicken that is, at least, one-year-old is known as a **cock** or a **rooster**. A group of three or more chickens is a **flock**.

A **purebred** is the offspring of two purebred parents that are of the same class, breed, and variety. A **hybrid** is a crossbreed of two species for the purpose of producing a chick with a unique set of characteristics. **Utility breeds** are chickens raised for the purpose of providing eggs and/or meat.

To further categorize chickens, a **dual-purpose** chicken is one that lays eggs but is also a meat chicken. A **meat bird** is exactly as the name implies. The meat bird is bred to grow quickly and has a broad chest for more meat.

Standard chickens are the larger chickens of standard breeds. They usually weigh in at anywhere from about five pounds up to 14 or 15 pounds. Smaller versions of a standard breed are called **bantams or banties** and weigh in at around two to four pounds. People who do not have much space in their chicken coop may opt for banties. Be aware, however, that banties' eggs will be a little smaller than the standard size hens will produce.

There are hundreds of different types of chickens. Purebred chickens are categorized according to class, breed, and variety. The **class** is the broadest category. The class refers to the region where the chickens were originally bred or traditionally associated. Classes of chickens include the following: Asiatic, American, Continental, Mediterranean, English, Oriental, and Miscellaneous.

Within classes of chickens is the **breed** of chicken. Chickens are categorized into breeds based on their similar features, markings, and body type. The various breeds include standard breeds and bantam breeds. Some of the most common breeds include the following:

American Breeds such as Jersey Giants, New Hampshire Red, Rhode Island Red, Plymouth Rock, Wyandotte

English Breeds such as Cornish, Orpington, Australorp, Dorking

Asiatic Breeds such as Cochin, Langshan, Brahma

Oriental Breeds such as Phoenix, Sumatra

Continental Breeds such as Houdan, Polish, Hamburg

Miscellaneous Breeds such as Araucana, Ameraucana, Frizzle

The Best Laying Breeds and Meat Breeds

If you're set on getting as many eggs as feasible from your chickens, you should know that some breeds are more prolific layers than others. The very best laying breeds can lay around 300 eggs per year in the right environment, with most of the best breeds laying around 250 eggs per year. Leghorn, Ancona, Fayoumi, Minorca, and Norwegian Jaerhon are among the best laying breeds. Other excellent layers include the following: Ameraucana, Ancona, Andalusian, Araucana, Australorp, Barred or Buff Rocks, Barnevelder, Campine, Catalana, Chantecler, Dominique, Delaware, Empordanesca, Fayoumi, Hamburg, Lakenvelder, Leghorn, Marans, Minorca, Norwegian Jaerhon, Orpingtons, Penedesenca, Plymouth Rock, Red or Black Star, Rhode Island Red, Rhode Island White, Silver Spangled Hamburg, Sussex, and Welsumer.

Some of the best meat breeds or dual purpose breeds are as follows: Barred Plymouth Rock, Buff Orpingtons, White Cornish, Delaware, White Leghorn, Red Ranger, Black Jersey Giant, New Hampshire Red, Rhode Island Red, Wyandottes, and White Rocks.

This is a very short list of laying hens and meat chickens. There are plenty of chicken breeds to choose from to keep fresh meat and eggs on your menu.

Dual purpose chickens allow you to get a decent number of eggs *and* meat from the same chicken. Some good considerations for dual purpose chickens are Delaware, Brahma, Rhode Island Red, Orpington, Araucana, Wyandotte, and Black Jersey Giant.

Other Considerations for Choosing Chickens

Besides choosing chickens that are best for eggs and meat, you need to consider the climate where you live. Some breeds are more sensitive to hot or cold weather. High humidity affects some breeds and can definitely affect mold and bacterial growth in the chicken coop. As an example, standard breeds don't fare well in extremely hot climates but can withstand colder winters. However, bantams can tolerate hot summers but do not like cold winters. Those who live in the South, Southeast, or Southwest where the summers are hot should consider bantams while those who live in northern states with milder summers and colder winters should consider standards. Of course, there are ways to insulate chicken coops and keep the chickens more comfortable if you live in an area with extreme temperatures. (We will discuss more about coops in a later section of this guide.)

If you have a limited amount of space and a small coop, the number of chickens you can keep is limited, but the size of the chickens matters also. Obviously, the smaller bantams are more suited to limited space in a small coop than the larger standards. However, the smaller bantams are better escape artists since they can fit into small spaces in a fence, so if you have a fence with gaps that a smaller chicken could fit through, the standard breed might be best for you.

Your budget for chickens and their habitat, feed, and supplies may determine what chickens you choose. The price of chickens can vary from breed to breed and from one part of the country to another.

Lastly, if you want to keep chickens because you want your children or grandchildren to experience a bit of farm life, the tradition of gathering eggs from the nest boxes, and learn to take responsibility for living animals, choose a breed that is calm and smaller. Large chickens may have a tendency to "boss" or dominate small children. This can be terrifying to toddlers and create a raucous in the chicken run. (Do not allow small children to carry food, such as a cookie or sandwich, around chickens as the birds will think the child is offering to share it with them.)

Chicks or Hens?

You must decide whether you'll start with chicks, fully grown chickens, or both. Another option is to buy fertile eggs and let them hatch. All of these options have advantages and disadvantages and the best choice will depend on your budget, time commitment, chicken set up, and intention for your chickens.

It is true that it takes more time to set up for and care for newly hatched chicks. Nonetheless, if you have the right set up and time, it's best to buy chicks instead of pullets and hens. When you raise a chick, you won't miss out on the hen's first egg-laying season, which is the best of her life. You'll also know what the hen has been eating all of its life and the quality of the eggs it is providing. Additionally, hens that have been a part of the same flock since chicks seem to be calmer around each other.

For the initial purchase, buying young chicks is less expensive than purchasing laying hens. But you have to consider that you'll also be buying feed for those chicks for a longer period and you have to be set up properly for chicks to stay warm and safe. As sad as it is, chicks can be susceptible to and succumb easily to disease. The cost of chicks lost must be factored into the overall cost of raising chickens.

If you decide to go with purchasing baby chicks and you live in a rural area, you may be able to buy chicks from a local farmer who has extras or a feed supply store that brings them in for sale in early spring. This can be exciting, especially for children, because you actually get to see the chicks and hand pick them. This also gives you the opportunity to inspect the chicks and make sure they are healthy. When you buy chicks from a local feed store, chances are the chicks are sexed—meaning they have been determined to be either male or female. This can be advantageous because it is difficult for a novice to know if they are getting male or female chicks. This is particularly true of small bantam chickens.

In many areas of the country, you can purchase baby chicks in the spring for as little as one to three dollars each. This is considerably less than six to ten dollars or more each for grown hens. Look for special sales on chicks at farm supply stores and feed stores in March or April. The stores run the promotional sales on chicks as a leader for selling feeders, waterers, feed, and other chick supplies. If the local farm and ranch store doesn't sell chicks, they may be able to direct you to a local farmer who does sell them. If you have a local farmers' market, you can ask vendors where you might find chicks or hens for sale. The market vendors may also be savvy to locals who build and sell chicken coops if you are in the market for one. Another way to possibly find out where to buy local chickens is to check around at the barn animal exhibits at the annual county fair.

If you live in a rural area, check with local 4-H clubs to see if there are 4-H members who may have chickens for sale. 4-H students are usually very knowledgeable about their animals and raise healthy ones. You may be able to find local 4-H groups through your school district office or check the listings at this site: http://www.4-h.org/contact/.

If you live in an urban area where there are no local farmers or feed supply stores, you can order your chicks and supplies from a hatchery and have them shipped to you. This is a viable option and it's quite fun to hear the lively peeping coming from inside the box when you receive them. When you order chicks from a hatchery, the minimum order for shipping is usually anywhere from 15 to 25 chicks depending on the time of year. Ordering in these quantities is for the safety of the new born chicks, though it is a fact that some of the chicks may not arrive alive. For this reason, most hatcheries will throw in a few extra chicks to compensate for any losses. Chick suppliers use special containers that are ventilated and most mail-order companies send newly-hatched chicks that can arrive at your local pick-up destination within 48 hours or less of your order. Keep in mind that hatcheries may have restrictions on when they will ship chicks. This means they will not ship chicks to some regions during the months that are too cold or too hot for the chicks to survive the trip. (Interesting side note: just before baby chicks hatch, they consume the egg sacks' nutrition thus enabling them to survive the shipping process.)

If you type "mail order chickens" or "chicken hatcheries" into your Internet browser, you can find plenty of hatcheries. Don't forget to check the reviews from customers who have bought chickens from the hatcheries that you are considering. You can also find hatchery advertisements in farm and homesteading magazines. Visiting a 4-H chicken barn at the county fair or a livestock auction at your local fairgrounds can give you an idea of what various breeds of chickens look like so you can be better prepared when you order.

Chicken breeders have the option of becoming National Poultry Improvement Plan (NPIP) certified. This means the breeder should follow certain guidelines for healthy chickens including having their facilities and chickens checked annually for serious diseases.

How Many Chickens Do I Need?

Some people determine the number of hens they keep by the number of eggs they want to collect each day. Most hens will lay one egg approximately every 24-26 hours except during the winter months of short, dark days when there will be no eggs because chickens require 15 hours of the sunshine per day to produce eggs. Keep in mind that, depending on the breed, some chickens do not lay eggs every day and may only lay one egg every third day.

If you're keeping chickens primarily for meat instead of eggs, your flock number should, to some extent, be determined by how many chickens you need to keep chicken dinners on the table and in the freezer. If you think you'll be gifting friends, neighbors, or family members with chicken dinners, count those as part of your flock. When considering numbers, remember that your chickens may be smaller in weight than the store-bought chickens that are given growth hormones to make them fatter. If your family requires a six-pound chicken for a meal, you may need to count two of your smaller chickens for one meal. Besides, who doesn't want leftover cold chicken for lunch the next day?

The available space in your hen house for sleeping perches and nest boxes will also determine how many hens you can keep. As a general rule, you will need about two square feet of henhouse space per hen. It only takes a very small coop to easily house two to three hens.

Hens are social animals and it's best not to have just one. Of course, if you want fertile eggs to eat or to hatch, you must include at least one rooster in your chicken count. Roosters are very active in the chicken run, and they mate frequently. For the most part, they are not discriminatory and will mate with most of the hens, though there may be some hens who will try to refuse. If there are not enough hens for his liking, the rooster may tire the available hens with his frequent activity and cause damage to the hens' backs, combs, and necks with his spurs and beak. In general, a good ratio of roosters to hens is one rooster to every eight to ten hens.

Chicken owners who are not interested in having fertile eggs often skip having a rooster. Even though some hens can be aggressive, it's more likely for the rooster to be aggressive and create drama in the chicken run and chase, peck, and claw people when they are in the chicken run. This can be frightening for a child, particularly if they have not been taught how to handle a rude rooster that tries to dominate humans. If you choose an adult rooster, make sure you ask for one that is not aggressive. If you raise a rooster, you may not know of its aggressive nature until it's older.

Roosters aren't all bad. Besides fertilizing eggs, the rooster boasts another talent. He seems to feel it his duty to watch over and protect his hens. He will sound the alarm if he senses predators or other danger to the flock. The rooster puffing out his chest, flapping wings wildly, and giving a warning crow may be enough to keep predators out of the coop, or, at least, get your attention, before the predator can reach the hens.

As sad as it can be, chickens are often lost to predators or various diseases that can quickly wipe out most of a flock. Some can find a way out of their enclosures. All that said to say that it's best to have a few extra hens on board if you have space for them. If you have more eggs than you can use, your family, friends, and neighbors will be happy to help you out by taking the extras.

Choose Healthy Chickens

First and foremost, you want to choose chickens that are healthy. Bringing home chickens that are in any condition other than optimum health is throwing away your money and can dash your hopes of successfully keeping chickens because one sick chicken can quickly lead to a flock of sick (or dead) chickens. How do you know if chickens are healthy? Here are some general guidelines that you can use to check for healthy chickens:

Pay attention to the chicken's eyes. A healthy chicken has bright, alert eyes. The eyes should not be dull or weepy with fluid. If you lean in close to the chicken, you should not hear any sounds coming from the nostril area as they breathe in and out.

When a chicken is healthy, their wattle and comb look plump, as though it contains gel. The color of the comb and wattle should be brighter red and not too gray/white. The feathers should be a bit shiny and smooth rather than frizzy. A hen that looks like she just stuck her beak into an electrical socket has probably endured some illness or trauma. The feathers should amply cover the body without the skin showing in spots. Of course, feathers will be scarcer during their molting season when the chickens lose their old feathers and new ones are growing in. The feathers near the vent (the hole in the behind where the poop and egg come out) should be fairly clean and not be surrounded by excessive moisture.

Healthy chickens have a full, rounded breast, but the chicken shouldn't be inappropriately thin or fat. They strut and cluck and show a bit of attitude. They hold their heads high. While some chickens are calmer than others, a chicken that is completely sedentary and has a drooping head may be sick. Select chickens with sturdy legs that are not deformed.

If you check the environment of the chickens, you should take note of the droppings on the ground. The droppings of healthy chickens are firm and white-capped, not runny.

Thinking about bringing your healthy flock home can be exciting, and with the right preparations, can bring you joy for years to come. Read on to learn how to create the best home for your chickens.

Section 3: Create the Perfect Chicken World

You've probably seen the darling chicken coops that are styled and painted to look like princess castles, sweet gingerbread cottages, or classic red barns. They're super cute and fun to look at, but in reality, the chickens don't know the difference between those expensive coops and a coop fashioned from an old shed or repurposed scrap material gathered from here and there. In other words, the stylish chicken coops are designed for *people* to enjoy. If you can afford to do so and would enjoy the cute decorative chicken coops, go for it! But know that your chickens can be happy and safe with a lot less. In fact, you may already have elements of your chicken coop just collecting dust in the garage or shed. (There is plenty more information on how to obtain a coop later in this section.)

The Chicken Run

Chickens live a simple life, but they have a few shelter requirements that should be met for them to live a safe, good life. Chickens need a place to get out in the sunshine and squawk and scratch about for insects and worms during the day. Besides bringing them great satisfaction, chickens need exercise, and their scratching and darting about provides it. Some fortunate chickens have the run of the entire yard or acreage every day. This is ideal, but in most cases, chickens must be contained within certain areas for their own good and for the good of the humans with which they share the property. This may be particularly true if you are an urban chicken farmer. The enclosed area that hens and roosters use for their daily exercise and foraging is the **chicken run**. The chicken run can be a permanently fenced area where the chickens go from the henhouse into the yard when the coop door is opened in the morning or it can be a portable large "cage" without a bottom that is on wheels and can be moved around from one grassy spot to another every few days. The portable model is called a chicken tractor. A popular form of the chicken tractor is to build a henhouse on a platform with wheels and have rolls of chicken wire fencing attached that can quickly be extended and attached together to set up as a portable run.

The main function of the chicken run is to give the chickens plenty of space and access to the sunshine in an area where they are protected from predators and other dangers. The chicken run fence should be at least four-feet in height to keep the chickens from going over the top. Even though chickens do not really "fly" like most birds, they can become excited and run and leap into the air. If they get lucky, they might make it over a shorter fence. Chicken runs with an enclosed wire top provide added protection against escaping chickens and from wild predators or a stray cat or dog with less-than-noble motives.

(Tip: If you find yourself with a chicken that seems to consistently find its way over your fencing, clip a small section of each of its wings so that the feathers are uneven. This is an effective way to stop the escapee from escaping.)

Chicken runs are usually constructed of wood or metal posts and chicken wire or hog wire purchased at a farm or feed supply store or do-it-yourself hardware store. The posts should be evenly placed every four to six feet to keep the wire from sagging. They should be put about ten to twelve inches into the ground. For sturdier, permanent posts, you can pour cement around the posts in the ground. If you want a semi-permanent run that can be moved later, you can set the posts in a concrete cylinder that is about twelve inches tall and wide enough to be stable. A five-gallon bucket is just about perfect for doing this. If you don't opt to use cement, check the posts every once in a while to make sure they are still firmly planted.

Runs that are attached to the henhouse are stable and permanent and allow the hens to go directly into the henhouse without human help once the sun starts going down in the evening. You will find many different plans on the internet using lumber that combine both the chicken yard and coop for a more secure environment.

Grass and foliage are excellent for harboring the bugs that chickens like to forage for, but it doesn't take long for a larger flock to turn a grassy space into a dirt area. One of the benefits of having a portable chicken run is to move it from one spot to another before the grass in any one area is destroyed. To avoid mud in the run, you can use a layer of fine sand to cover the ground of the chicken run. Chickens actually roll around in the sand to bathe themselves.

Those who practice the permaculture method of gardening often park their chicken tractor on their garden after the garden has been put to bed for the fall so the chickens can fertilize the garden soil for the following spring.

You may want to opt for herbal or other ground covering for the chicken run. Planting ground cover creates a bug habitat that adds excitement to the chickens' day and helps keep mud to a minimal. It also gives the chickens added nutrition as they nibble on it. Tall plants such as sunflowers and Jerusalem artichokes make pretty organic fences around the outside of a permanent chicken run. The dried sunflower seeds from the sunflowers and the tubers from the Jerusalem artichokes provide free food for the chickens. You will find that having these extra plants for food can cut down on your chicken feed bill during the summer.

However, be aware that there are some plants that should NOT be planted in the chicken run or where chickens can get to them. Some of the more common plants to AVOID are as follows:

arum lily	azalea	bird of paradise
bishop's weed	bloodroot	bluebonnet
boxwood	buckthorn	burdock
castor bean	chalice (trumpet vine)	clematis
coriander	coffee bean	daffodil

daphnia	death camus	elderberry
elephant ear	eucalyptus	foxglove
some grasses such as Johnson	sorghum or broom corn	hemlock
holly	honeysuckle	horsetail
hoya	hyacinth	jasmine
juniper	larkspur	lily of the valley
milk vetch	lobelia	lupine
Mexican poppy	milkweed	mistletoe
monkshood	morning glory	myrtle
nettles	oleander	oxalis
parsley	pigweed	poinsettia
poison ivy	potato shoots	poison hemlock
ranunculus	rhubarb leaves	sorrel
sweet pea	tansy ragwort	tobacco
umbrella plant	hairy vetch	Virginia creeper
wisteria	yellow jasmine	

When in doubt, always identify and check whether plants in the chicken area are okay for chickens to consume because if it is within the chickens' reach, it will be pecked and nibbled on.

Wherever you put your chicken run, keep in mind that chickens poop *a lot and everywhere*. Anything, such as lawn furniture or children's outdoor toys are fair game. It matters not to them. Make sure to wash your hands after coming into contact with objects with chicken droppings on them.

Gardeners and chickens alike can benefit from chickens roaming in the garden eating bugs and leaving behind fertilizer, but chickens are not always well-behaved in the garden. They can trample plants and be overly zealous when it comes to eating the plants. Some gardeners section off a part of the garden that the hens can feed on without ruining other parts of the garden. And be aware that chicken manure runs hotter than other manures and can burn some plants.

The chickens' feed and water should be accessible to them in the chicken run rather than in the henhouse where it can be splashed and spilled and create moisture and mold issues in the bedding. Never place it under where the chickens roost at night. The waterer should provide ample water for the chickens on hot days when the hens will drink more to stay cool or for when you are unexpectedly kept from adding more water throughout the day. During the winter, you'll have to make sure the chickens' water doesn't freeze, leaving the flock without water. Sometimes this requires moving the waterer inside the henhouse and/or using special heated waterers that do not allow the water to freeze. (This happens more in the colder parts of the country.)

It's common to attach feeders and waterers to the fence posts to secure them. Keep in mind that if the feeders are accessible to the small paws of raccoons, mice, and other food-seeking animals, you may end up feeding unwanted guests that can keep your hens overly-excited and not laying eggs, at the very least.

There are many types of feeders and waterers including trough types and treadle types that are covered to keep the food dry until the chicken steps on the treadle to open the cover. The best thing to do is browse chicken supply catalogs or websites to determine the type that will work best for your setup and budget. Some chicken owners simply use tin pie pans for feeders or they get creative with making their own feeders from common materials found at do-it-yourself stores. Covered five-gallon buckets with holes drilled in the low end of the side (for the feed in the bucket to flow through into the dish) can be bolted to a shallow dish with a rim, then hung at a comfortable height for the chickens is a perfectly good feeder that keeps the food dry until it's in the dish. (See photo on the next page.) This feeder can then be hung from a rafter in the chicken yard a few inches above the ground. A feeder can also be created from PVC pipes secured to an outside wall of the henhouse or between two posts. There are many creative options for functional feeders that provide fresh, dry feed for the flock. A good source for creative ideas for feeders and waterers is www.pinterest.com.

The Henhouse

As the sun starts to set, your chickens will be ready to call it a day. Chickens are habitual creatures and their natural instinct is to go to a safe place, hop on their perch, and sleep until the sun starts to rise once again. The henhouse, which is the "house" part of the chicken coop and is often referred to as *the coop* even though the coop includes both the henhouse and the chicken run, also provides a place for chickens to find security when they feel threatened by danger or it gets too hot or too cold outside. Roosters also need a safe, dry place to sleep separately from the hens, but obviously do not have the same nesting and brooding needs as hens.

Hens prefer to be off the ground when they are sleeping. A henhouse on stilts is ideal, but not necessary. A henhouse on stilts can help keep predators out of the henhouse and keep the floor from absorbing moisture. Even if the henhouse is built on the ground, a subfloor should be put in, if possible, for warmth and to keep predators from digging through the ground to get in the henhouse. If the henhouse is not level with the ground, the hens will need a ramp to get in and out. Fat hens are not very athletic and can hurt themselves if they try to leap into the henhouse. An old ladder with rungs or wide board makes a great ramp for the henhouse.

The henhouse should provide about two square feet of space per hen. To keep your girls happy, you'll need to furnish the hen house with the following:

Perches: Hens like to sleep at least two to three feet above the ground or floor on perches, also called roosts, that are stationed close to the roof of the henhouse on walls other than where the nesting boxes are situated. This is an instinct that comes from when chickens were free range and used tree branches for their roosts. There should be about eight inches of perch space per chicken. During the summer months, hens need plenty of room around them for air circulation to stay cool. During the winter months, they may opt to roost closer together to share body heat. The perches should be about two inches in diameter so the hens can wrap their claws around them. Perches can be small tree branches or wooden dowels bought from a hardware store.

Nest boxes: For the hen to work her egg magic, she needs access to a nesting. The hen should be able to get into a nest box with just enough room to turn around in. The box is best if its off the ground at least 6 inches and filled with clean, dry nesting material such as straw, pine shavings, shredded newspaper or cardboard, or commercial bedding material made for animals. (Although the commercial bedding material can be expensive.) Make sure the bedding is completely dry and free of mold at all times. Wet, moldy bedding can breed bacteria that can make your hens sick. You can help keep the bedding in the nest mold-free by turning it daily so air can circulate around the bedding. Though some might say changing the bedding once a month is too often, doing so cuts the risk of bacterial illness and is well worth the effort and expense.

If you are able to place your nest boxes so they can be accessed from an outside door or opening, it will enable you to collect eggs without crawling around in the henhouse and getting dirty. This may not seem like a big deal in the beginning, but over the long term, it can save you a lot of time and effort.

There should be a minimum of one nest box for every four hens in the henhouse. The nest box should be about 12 inches deep and 18 inches tall and they should be spaced far enough apart and where one hen doesn't accidentally land on the eggs in another box when trying to reach her own box. If the boxes are too close and a hen accidentally breaks eggs, she may develop a taste for raw eggs. You can see what a nasty habit that would be, and once a hen develops the habit, it is very difficult to break them of it.

(Example of a newly made group nesting box that worked out well.)

Samantha H.

There should be just enough room in the box or basket for at least one-inch and preferably two inches, of bedding and a fat hen. If the nest box is too large, the hen will not feel secure, so bigger isn't better. Even though you might think the hen would want to stretch out and sleep in her comfy nesting box, that is not the case. Hens roost on perches and use the nesting box for laying eggs and keeping the eggs warm for hatching.

It cannot be said often enough that the dryness and cleanliness of the nest boxes and henhouse can be the health or death of a flock. With that in mind, when you consider your henhouse layout, remember that you will need to get inside the henhouse to clean and replace bedding. An access door that is large enough for a human to enter or bend or step over is necessary in order for the caretaker to do their work.

(Tip: Using clean 5-gallon buckets, with handles removed, fastened side by side and filled with nesting materials also works great.)

Is it Best to Buy or Build the Coop?

You have several options for acquiring your henhouse or coop. If you're fortunate, you may already have an old garden or tool shed or outbuilding that can easily and inexpensively be transformed into a henhouse. You can also buy a coop, hire a carpenter to build one for you, or build one yourself.

If you buy a pre-made coop or hire someone to build one for you, you will have to pay for labor that you could provide yourself if you're handy with a hammer and nails and can follow a simple design plan. However, if you have more cash than time for such projects, you may come out ahead buying a coop. A small coop/yard can take a minimum of a few days' time when you design/buy plans for the coop, shop for the materials, and build it (but can be oh so rewarding when you're finished and can show it off to your family and friends.)

If you purchase a coop that is large and you do not have a truck for transporting it to your property, you may have to rent a truck or enlist the help of a friend or family member with a truck. The same may be true if you purchase large sheets of plywood from the lumber yard, though many lumber yards offer free delivery if you order a certain dollar amount of building material or charge a small fee for delivery if your order falls below the minimum to qualify for free delivery.

Just a reminder that if you are part of a neighborhood association or house development, there may be specific restrictions on the size of the henhouse and the materials and paint used. So before you buy or build, make sure you know what is allowable on your property. In some counties, you may be required to get a building permit if you build anything more than a very portable henhouse on your property.

Find or buy the best building material you can afford and paint or stain the henhouse to help weatherproof it. You'll want your chicken coop to withstand the brutal beating of the hens and winter/summer weather conditions for many years to come. Choose certain times of the year, such as spring and fall, to weatherize, clean, and repair your coop so that it will serve many future flocks without rotting or falling apart.

Coop Design and Set-up

As long as the functional elements of a henhouse are in place, you can use your imagination when choosing a coop design. You can determine if you want a henhouse on stilts or closer to the ground, what size door you want, whether you want windows, and whether you want a plain or stylish abode for your hens. Some chicken owners enjoy designing a henhouse that looks like a miniature version of their own house. Gingerbread house style cottages, English garden cottages, and barn designs are also popular.

Safety and ventilation should be the two major functional considerations for your design. Hens may put up a fight with flapping their wings and clucking, but they are not warriors. To keep your hens safe from predators, make sure that your design does not allow gaps or openings that cats, dogs, mice, skunks, badgers, foxes, coyotes, and raccoons can fit through.

To keep the hens' enemies from digging underneath the chicken run fence, dig a twelve-inch deep trench into the ground to bury the fence wire. Placing large rocks or heavy logs along the bottom of the buried fence wire adds another deterrent to determined diggers.

Your coop should be built or placed on an area that is well-drained so the chickens are not subjected to standing in water when they go out for exercise. Additionally, it will be much easier on you not to have to deal with water puddles when tending to the chickens. A porch cover or awning can give the chickens a place to run to stay dry during spring and summer rain showers when they might not want to be inside the henhouse.

If you live in an area with very hot summers, consider building the coop in a spot underneath or near a large tree that can provide extra shade for the chickens. If you do this, keep low-hanging branches completely trimmed so the chickens do not use them for roosting or to escape the chicken run.

A coop that is built off the ground also provides an extra layer of security from predators and allows for better air flow on hot summer nights.

Vents that can be opened and closed should also be installed at the top of the henhouse for better air circulation. Small windows with glass that can be opened and shut, or openings that are covered with a screen in the summer and metal or rubber flaps or other material in the winter can also help provide air flow.

As stated previously, hens need 15 hours of sunlight per day to produce eggs. During the winter, when the days are short, some chicken farmers use artificial lighting in the form of barn lamps in the henhouse to "trick" the hens' bodies into producing eggs. Glass windows that allow the sun to shine into the henhouse can also help with the hens' laying cycle and give you a way to spy on your chickens without entering the henhouse.

To recap, your coop design and set-up should be practical, fit your budget, keep your chickens protected, and meet their needs for comfort and functionality. If you can accomplish that, you're good to go!

Kathy Libby

Section 4: Get to Know Your Chickens

No matter why you raise chickens or how determined you are to view them as simple egg and meat providers, if you're like most chicken owners, you will grow fond of your flock. As you observe them and take care of them, you will learn what is normal for them. If you spend much time with them, you'll start to recognize each hen by their personality as much as by their coloring, size, and breed. Do not be shocked if you start to call them by name! (Tip: you might want to avoid naming chickens you or your family will be eating in the future.)

In addition to getting to know your chickens, you need to know *about* chickens, in general, to satisfy your curiosity and cut down on any anxiety you may have about whether you'll be a good and responsible chicken owner. Knowing about chickens can be a lifesaver if your flock gets sick or if you wonder why your hens are behaving in an odd manner. Your flock deserves the best, so get to know as much as you can about chickens and give them the best.

The Chicken's Anatomy

If you know the parts of a chicken's body, you will have an easier time talking to a vet or farmer if your chickens get sick or go through something abnormal.

Here are the main body parts of a chicken and the definition for each part:

Oviduct: the reproductive tunnel of the hen that consists of the infundibulum, magnum, isthmus, uterus, and vagina. The egg slides through the oviduct to come out at the vent.

Vent: the orifice in the chicken's behind where poop and the hens' eggs come out.

Comb: the red fleshy protrusion that is on top of the chicken's head. Hens and roosters both have combs, but often the rooster's comb is bigger and more noticeable.

Beak: the extended cover of the chicken's mouth. (No, chickens do not have teeth!)

Mandibles: the upper and lower part of the chicken's beak.

Beard: the feathers in a small clump under the chicken's beak

Cape: the feathers that are between the neck and shoulder of a chicken.

Barring: the stripes of two different colors across a chicken's feathers

Self-color: single color all over the chicken's body

Saddle: the chicken's back (located in front of the tail)

Shank: the part of the chicken's leg that is located between the thigh and the foot of the chicken. On the human body, we might refer to the shank as the shin.

Wattle: the wobbly part that hangs on each side of the chicken's beak. The wattle helps keep the chicken cooler when the weather is hot. Roosters and hens have wattles, but the hen's wattle is usually smaller than the roosters. Most chickens have red wattles but some, such as the Silkie, have purple wattles.

Spurs: the sharp growths on the roosters and some hen's legs. (No, not the basketball team!)

Parson's nose: the lump of flesh that sprout the chicken's tail feathers.

Sexing

With chicks, the gender is not obvious. It can be almost impossible to know the gender of a chick unless you are a professional in the process of determining the gender, which is known as *sexing*. And yes, sexing is a real job. If a chicken owner is not concerned about the sex of their chickens, they can choose from the straight-run category offered by most hatcheries, which are chickens that have not had professional sexing and their gender is unknown. Feed stores may offer chicks in sexed and straight-run categories. Straight-run chicks cost less as the owner doesn't know if they will end up with more hens or more roosters. City dwellers that are not allowed to keep roosters should only buy sexed chicks so they know they are only getting females. However, be aware that sexing is not infallible. Sometimes a rooster will sneak by even the best of professionals.

If you are interested in learning sexing, check out an animal husbandry book from the public library or contact your county extension agency to see if they have a library with animal husbandry books for detailed information.

Chicken Society and Habits

Chickens are social animals and have developed a method or "government" for living together in a flock. You've heard the term "pecking order?" In each flock or sub-flock, there is a lead rooster and one lead hen. The lead rooster is in charge of the flock and controls them. The other chickens follow the leaders but also have a pecking order amongst themselves. The leaders get to eat and drink first when at the feeder and waterer and all the other chickens know the leaders are the bosses. However, young cockerels will try to exert dominance over the other young chicks, and as the chicks get a bit older, other chicks will challenge the cockerel's dominance. The roosters may face each other with their heads down and their neck feathers ruffled. If both roosters are determined and neither backs down, the roosters may spar or fight. Sometimes they spar until one is dead, though they usually stop before then. If the challenger is successful, there will be a new leader. If the challenger is not successful, the leader retains his position in the flock. The loser of the challenge may go off alone and try to establish his own sub-flock.

With the well-established pecking order in a flock, it can sometimes be a bit difficult to bring new chickens into the flock. You either have to have a closed flock that you do not add to or go through the process of new chickens being accepted into the flock. When you bring in new hens, quarantine them as far away from your flock as possible before you let them enter the chicken run or henhouse. Even if you got them from a reputable local farm, chickens can be carriers of disease that they do not succumb to until they are in a new environment and stressed by the move and changes involved. If the chickens suddenly become sick, they will spread the disease to your established flock. It's best to leave the new chickens quarantined for from 14 up to 30 days to lower the risk of your flock being wiped out by disease. This also gives the new chickens time to settle down and acclimate to their new environment.

When you are ready to take the new chickens out of quarantine, you can make the transition easier by putting them in a smaller cage or partition off part in the chicken run. That way, the new chickens can be introduced through a barrier to the established flock. The chickens may squawk at each other and try to peck each other, but you can intervene and let them know they have to learn to get along. You can make the same gentle transition when introducing the new chickens to the henhouse.

Roosters will also try to establish their dominance over you. It's important for you to let the rooster know that you are in charge. This is best done when the rooster is young. You can help them understand that you are higher than they are in the pecking order by breaking up their dominant behavior when they try to exhibit it. For instance, if the rooster is trying to get to a hen step in between the dominant rooster and the hen to let him know that you have the authority and physical power to stop him.

Believe it or not, when roosters crow, it's not just to wake you up. Roosters actually crow to communicate with their flock and make their presence known to predators. Hens may sound like they are just squawking all the time, but they are also communicating. You may notice that broody hens with new chicks order the chicks around while she is teaching them to come to her when called. The chicks recognize the tone of their mother hen's voice.

As you watch your chickens, you will continue to learn their habits. When they act a certain way or do a certain move, you will begin to understand exactly what it means. You will certainly enjoy their individual personalities and antics. If you see your chickens scratch a hole in the ground and use their wings and feet to throw up dirt, it is bath time! The dirt attracts and clears away the excess oil from the feathers and also loosens and rids the feathers of parasites. Your chickens will probably bathe once every day or every few days.

Molting

One of the changes that your hens and roosters will go through as the days get cooler and shorter is molting. Some hens lose the majority of their feathers all at once and it can take up to three or more months for them to completely grow back. This can be alarming if you don't know what is going on. The hens are not at their best-looking self when they are molting. Other hens lose a few feathers at a time and grow in new feathers a few at a time so the process doesn't seem as severe. Molting starts at the chicken's head and neck, goes to the breast and back, then to the thighs, legs, and tail feathers. The new feathers that grow in, called pin feathers, grow in the same succession.

Molting is natural and doesn't make your chickens sick in any way. They may look haggard with the absence of feathers during molting, but if your chickens seem sick during molting, they probably are sick and need your immediate attention.

Typically, hens stop laying during molting. Their body uses their daily nutrients for the molting process instead of the egg process. During molting, making sure that your hens receive plenty of non-meat protein

28

sources is important. You can accomplish this by adding cottage cheese to their diet. Hens seem to love cottage cheese, or perhaps they just know that their bodies need it during certain stages of their life. Or you can buy a commercially prepared, high-protein food with vitamins and minerals to use during this time. When molting, put out extra feed so the hens can enjoy extra meals when they choose to do so.

During molting, it's best to let your chickens rest and not do anything that might stress them, such as moving them to a new coop or bringing new chickens into the flock. Take extra care to make sure there are no lurking predators to terrorize the flock and do not let neighborhood dogs or cats harass them. It's best to avoid handling chickens during molding as it can be stressful and painful for them. If your children have a habit of picking up their favorite hen to say good morning, explain to them that they'll need to temporarily place the habit on hold.

The Fundamentals of Feeding

Hens like to forage for their food. In their foraging, they feed on bugs and plants that should be considered as treats but not their only food. Chickens need a solid two meals per day for optimum health and vitality. Their meals should consist of the correct balance of protein, carbohydrates, minerals, vitamins, and fiber. The easiest and most certain way to ensure your hens get a balanced diet is to purchase commercially prepared chicken feed that is sold at animal feed stores or can be ordered online. This takes the guesswork out of whether your chicken is getting everything they need. Chickens that are fed only table scraps and allowed to forage will probably survive, but may not thrive.

You can get chicken feed in various forms that include pellets, crumbs, or mash. What you feed the chicken depends largely on the chicken's age and the current state of health or stage in life. Chicks should definitely be fed commercial chick crumbs to get a good start on life. The chick crumbs provide the appropriate amount of protein, vitamins, and minerals for the chick's growth and development during the crucial first months of life. Malnourished chicks easily succumb to sickness and death.

As the chicks reach the pullet stage, their nutritional needs will change from chick crumbs to a commercial mixture for pullets. The pullet mixture includes grit. Grit is minuscule gravel that pullets and hens need with their food to grind the feed while it is in the chicken's gizzard. Chickens do not have teeth and cannot chew their food. The grit in the gizzard does the "chewing" for them. It's important to always keep a small dish of grit available for your chickens. Chickens can become sick and die if they can't properly digest their food. Put the grit in a container that will keep it dry.

At around the four to five-month mark, the young chickens have developed into plump, round hens and are fully-feathered. This is the time to start transitioning to feed that has extra calcium for the laying hen. You can do this over a few weeks by gradually decreasing the pullet feed and replacing it with hen feed until, after a few weeks, you are feeding only hen feed.

You can supplement commercial food with some table scraps such as bits of fruit, greens, and small amounts of protein such as cottage cheese or yogurt. People seem to love to feed chickens bread, but a little goes a long way and should not be fed constantly. Chickens, like people, can become obese if they eat too many calories, and particularly of the white flour version. The gizzard can become clogged if the chicken eats large amounts of food in a short period of time. Chickens that maintain a good weight are healthier and more mobile. (Such as is the case with humans.)

When providing bits of healthy food for the hens, remember that some foods can start to decay quickly and contain enough moisture to create a breeding ground for mold. Pick up rotting food from the chicken run every day when you feed. Teach children not to throw food into the chicken run without asking permission first. Foods that can safely be fed to chickens include chard, spinach, leaf lettuce, tomatoes, small amounts of pasta, berries, small chunks of fruit, herb leaves, small chunks of bread, fresh corn, and small amounts of cottage cheese and yogurt.

Some act as though chickens are animal garbage disposals and can be fed any and everything, but chickens should not be fed moldy or rotten food, heavily salted or spicy food, junk food such as potato chips, or fried foods. Feeding garlic and cabbage can make the hens' eggs have a bad odor. Raw potato peels are difficult for the chickens to digest.

If you've ever observed hens, you know they love to scratch in the dirt. While this may seem to be their primary source of entertainment, it serves the purpose of surfacing treats from the ground. During the cold winter months when worms and bugs aren't as plentiful, your chickens will enjoy scratch strewn about in the chicken run. Scratch is a mixture of cracked grains and corn that can be purchased at the feed store. Scratch adds a bit of needed extra starch during the cold winter months, but it is not to be considered as a meal.

201122

How Do Hens Make Eggs?

Now you know a little more about a chicken's body, but perhaps you're still wondering how hens make eggs. Really, when you think about it, it's pretty amazing!

At the sign of the first sunlight in the morning, your hens will wake up and start to bustle about. The light signals the hens' pituitary gland that it's time to lay an egg. That is why hens lay very little or not at all during the dark winter months—there are not enough daylight hours to signal to the pituitary gland. Some chicken owners get around this natural function by putting lamps with 40-watt bulbs in them about seven feet off the ground in the henhouse to provide the necessary 15 hours per day of light. Others prefer to give their hens the winter off and wait for natural sunlight to trigger the hen's laying season.

Laying hens need to remain calm and have an adequate diet to consistently lay eggs. Most hens produce an egg every 24 to 26 hours, though some will lay only three or four times per week. There is no set time of day that chickens lay their eggs, but as a rule they don't usually lay them in the late evening or at night.

Not all hens follow form and lay their eggs in a nesting box. It isn't uncommon for at least one or two to go rogue and find a bush or other private place to lay their eggs. It's best to deter this behavior when you can. Otherwise, you'll have a treasure hunt on your hands every day. Not to say that can't be fun at times, especially for children.

What happens between the hen and the sunny-side-up egg on your breakfast plate? Biology and animal husbandry books offer detailed information on how the egg forms, but here is the short version that explains the basics of how your chicken provides you with eggs:

> A young female chicken has two ovaries, but the right ovary immediately begins to shrivel. This is the signal for the left ovary to go into action so the eggs can form and exit the hen's body. The active left ovary contains about 4,000 undeveloped egg yolks called ova. When the chicken is anywhere between 17 and 32 weeks old, the ova starts to form yolk layers and mature. They mature one after another, and the mature ova slide into the oviduct of the hen's body, which is the long tunnel that ends in the vent of the hen. When a hen has been active with a rooster, the egg may be fertilized with sperm as it goes through the oviduct. If not, the egg will be an ordinary egg. When a chick isn't in the picture, the unfertilized yolk is surrounded by albumen, which is the egg white. The yolk is wrapped in fibers that secure it in the egg white so it doesn't blend together and then is enclosed in the eggshell. The egg continues through the hen's body and comes out the vent (hole in the behind) of the hen. Once in a while, you'll discover in your egg collecting an egg that came through the vent without much of a shell layer to it.

When you crack freshly laid eggs that you've gathered from your henhouse, you may sometimes see a spot of blood in the egg. This is called a *meat spot* and is harmless. It is caused by a blood vessel breaking when the egg begins to form and does not affect the quality of the egg. Though it may not seem very appetizing, the egg is still perfectly edible. You may also see string-like "cords" on each side of the egg yolk. It may seem logical to think that these stringy pieces are the beginning formation of a chick, but they are not. This is called chalazae and are the cords that hold the yolk centered in the egg.

All eggs contain a light-colored tiny spot in the center of the yolk. This spot is called the germinal disc. When eggs are fertile and incubated, the baby chick develops from the germinal disc. Examining the germinal disc can let you determine if an egg is fertile or not. When it is fertile, the germinal disc will have an extra ring around it.

You can see why the simple chicken requires proper care and nutrition in order for her body to do the work to produce eggs. What an amazing system! And perhaps that is a huge part of the fascination with chickens.

If the hen has contact with the rooster, the egg story changes and ends with the hatching of baby chicks. There is information on how to raise chicks in the next section.

Should You Wash and Refrigerate Fresh Eggs?
When you gather eggs from the nest boxes, sometimes they may be dirty, have feathers stuck to them, and have poop on them. While this is not exactly appetizing, it does not hurt the egg. (And if the nesting boxes are kept clean, the dirty eggs will be fewer.) Try to ignore what they look like and think about how organically nutritious and delicious they are! This does, however, bring up a question that chicken owners debate: Should you wash the fresh eggs or not?

Egg shells are porous, but they have a micro membrane coating on them, which is called the *bloom*, to protect them from bacteria and keep them clean. The bloom is for the protection of the baby chick that could be growing on the other side of the shell, but all eggs have the bloom even if they aren't fertile eggs. So rest assured that the mess on the outside of the egg shell doesn't usually contaminate the unwashed egg. Unwashed eggs will remain fresh longer than washed eggs.

However, when you wash the egg, the bloom is removed. At that point, after the bloom is removed, bacteria can find its way through the porous eggshell and into the egg so you must take precautions. If you wash your eggs use WARM water, not cool or cold, as the cold water can aid in drawing water into the eggshell.

Before the eggs are washed, they do not necessarily have to be refrigerated if they will be used within about a week or so of gathering them, and some do not refrigerate their fresh eggs at all. This may seem very foreign to most people who have been taught to always refrigerate eggs. Store-bought eggs from commercial farms in the United States must be refrigerated because of the unnatural practices used to raise the chickens and harvest, transport, and store the eggs. In other countries, where natural farming practices are used, eggs are not usually refrigerated, and people leave them sitting on their counter for a few weeks. Take note that the longer an egg sits out, the more of it evaporates.

Chicken eggs come in various sizes and colors, depending on the breed and what they eat. The brown, beige, green, and blue eggs are beautiful to look at, but the nutritional value of colored eggs is no higher than that of white eggs and they do not taste any different than white eggs. The thing that can change the taste of an egg is what a chicken has eaten.

Whether organic chicken eggs are nutritionally better than commercial farm chicken eggs has been an ongoing debate for a while, but there is sufficient evidence to show that eggs from free-range chickens are more nutritional. In a 2007 egg-testing project, *Mother Earth News* compared pastured chicken eggs with the U.S. Department of Agriculture (USDA) nutrient data for commercial eggs. The pastured chicken eggs were found to contain one-third less cholesterol, one-fourth less saturated fat, three times more vitamin E, two times more omega-3 fatty acids, and seven times more beta-carotene. (http://articles.mercola.com/sites/articles/archive/2011/09/02/why-does-this-commonly-vilified-food-actually-prevent-heart-disease-and-cancer.aspx).

So now you know the basics about your chickens and the eggs they lay. When you get your chickens, keeping a journal can be a good idea. As an example, assign one or two journal pages to each chicken. Take a picture of that chicken and tape it to their assigned page. Make notes as you observe the chicken. Note when they start laying, how often they lay, and what color and size their eggs are. Note when they become sick, their behavior changes, or about their habits. This can be beneficial for yourself and also if you need to "train" someone to watch after your chickens if you have to be away from home for a few days. And who knows, perhaps your chicken journal will someday turn into a fun book about chickens!

S A Slack, Author

Section 5: Raising Chicks

When a hen sits on her fertile eggs to keep them warm until they hatch, she knows exactly what to do to protect those eggs, bring her chicks into the world, and provide what they need. These hens are said to have gone *broody*, and even if they have none of their own eggs, they are perfectly happy to sit on another hen's **clutch** (a group of eggs.) They may also incubate eggs that are not fertile. After all, it's in her nature to be a "mother hen." Hens that go broody usually do so in the spring, after they has molted in the fall or early winter and grown back their feathers.

You may be able to tell when one of your hens have gone broody because she will usually choose the most private nest box in the henhouse and settle into it like it's her own, refusing to forsake the box entirely, only leaving the nest for short times before the incubation period starts. She will lay a clutch of from one to around ten eggs and sit on them, even if they are not fertile, but for her sake (and yours) hopefully they are. If another hen lays eggs in the broody hen's chosen nesting box, she will sit on their eggs, too. Once all of the eggs have been laid in the nest, the incubation process starts and the hen sits on the eggs for 21 days. During this time, the smart hens realize that some of her eggs were laid several days before the last eggs were laid, but she wants all of her chicks to hatch within about a 24-hour period. Therefore, she rolls the eggs around in the nest to adjust the amount of heat they get from her to help hasten or delay the development of the embryo. She also rolls the eggs so the embryo does not stick to the shell.

The broody hen is a busy hen about a very important business! She usually only leaves the nest one time a day to drink water, eat, and poop. It's important for her to have her own food and water close by, as she may resist leaving the nest if she has to go very far for her needs. During her broody time, it's important for her to stay healthy.

Part of the broody hen's business is to protect her eggs. She may aggressively hiss and attack other hens or humans who come near her eggs. She may even eat the embryo if she feels they are threatened with serious danger from an outsider. It's imperative to provide as much protection as you can for the broody hen. When possible, isolate her from the other hens and make sure she is safe from dogs, cats, and other predators that might approach her.

As the eggs begin to hatch, the broody hen will stay on the nest for up to three days, which is how long the chicks can go without receiving outside food or water. (As explained earlier, this is how hatcheries can safely send baby chicks through the mail as long as they are kept warm.)

Before the chicks arrive, whether they are hatched in your henhouse or purchased, you will need to set up a brooder for the baby chicks. The brooder can be a separate small room or a small part of a room that has been partitioned and is free of drafts (and any danger of predators), a box built for the chicks, a heavy-duty plastic bin, or even a large cardboard box with high walls. The brooder needs to have enough space for the number of chicks it will house to move around freely, but not be so big that it is difficult to keep heated. In general, about a half square foot of space for each chick will do the trick until the chicks are over two weeks old. Your household bathtub makes a perfect chicken starter and is easy to control the environments temperature with the raising and lowering of the bath rod...as long as you have an alternative place to bathe for a few weeks.

The brooder must also have a *safe* heat source to keep the chicks warm. Safety with the heat is a big issue. You don't want your brooder or henhouse to catch on fire because of faulty or unsafe heat sources. You can purchase a heater made specifically for the brooder or you can use a heat lamp or two with 85- to 125-watt bulbs that keep the temperature at a comfortable 95 degrees Fahrenheit about two inches off the floor until the outdoor temperature and brooder temperature are the same. But remember, DON'T place the lamps where they are too close to the bedding materials or can fall into bedding and catch it on fire. The lamps put off considerable heat and the bedding is perfect fodder for starting a fire. Be cautious of where you hang the heat lamps if you use a plastic brooder box.

It is recommended to use red bulbs when they are available in the required wattage. The red bulbs are easier on the chicks' eyes and do not agitate the chicks and cause them to peck at each other.

Even though it is sometimes recommended to use a heating pad on the brooder floor to keep the chicks cozy, it can present a worrisome problem. If the chicks become too hot, they have no place to escape to cool off. Overheated chicks do not survive. Be careful if you use this method.

It's a good idea to keep a thermometer in the brooder so you can adjust the temperature as needed. Place it a few inches above the brooder floor with strong tape or other sturdy method to be sure proper heat is reaching the chicks at this level. Keep the brooder temperature at 95 degrees Fahrenheit for the first seven to ten days and then start dropping it by about five degrees every week thereafter. You can also tell if your chicks are warm enough because they will look calm and content. If they are too warm, they will move to the walls and press against them. If they are too cold, they will huddle together.

The chicks need food and water in the brooder. Depending on how many chicks you have, a one-quart waterer and feeder are a good size to use. Make sure the waterer does not leak and that the chicks cannot become wet from the waterer. Cool moving air and wet chicks are not a good combination!

During their first moments of life, until all of the eggs are hatched, the chick eats off the yolk inside the shell. When the yolk is gone and the chicks are moved to the brooder, you need to provide them with chick starter crumble. The chick starter crumble comes in medicated and non-medicated varieties. The medicated crumble contains a coccidiostat, which helps prevent coccidiosis. Coccidiosis is one of the most prevalent chick diseases. However, if you're raising completely organic chickens, you'll want to buy the non-medicated chick crumble. As long as your brooder is cleaned daily to keep bacteria at bay and your chicks are not exposed to sick chickens or cold drafts, chicks usually do fine without medicated crumble. Check with the feed store or hatchery where you purchase your chicks for their specific recommendations when making your decision.

In the brooder, for the first few days, sprinkle the chick crumble on the floor so the chicks can see it. After that use chick feeders for the chicks, instead of regular feeders, so the chicks cannot fit into the small openings and poop in their food. This helps cut down on bacterial growth in the food. If you do have a hen in with your chicks, hang or place the hen's feeder and waterer high enough so the hen can comfortably reach them but the chicks cannot.

Chicks can become dehydrated fairly quickly and they usually do not survive dehydration, so it's important that their water dish not ever run dry. When you place the chicks in the brooder, gently dip their beak into the water so they know where to find the water. Mixing in a little vitamin/mineral powder made specifically for chicks can help their systems stay in a healthy balance.

Day-old chicks have wobbly legs and cannot walk well on a slippery surface. With that in mind, for the first four or five days, it's a good idea to cover the floor with something that allows them to get traction such as a sheet of rubberized drawer lining or paper towels. After the chicks' legs are stronger, switch to soft, absorbent litter for the floor. It's important not to use cedar litter, as it can be harmful to chickens. It's also absolutely mandatory that you keep the litter clean and dry. It's better to change it too often than not enough and risk bacterial growth that can cause sickness and death.

Your chicks will sleep a lot for the first six to eight days until they start to eat more and gain more energy for running around.

Observe your chicks often. Make sure they are not stressed. Common stress factors are the chicks not having enough water, being too cold, being too hot, or being suddenly frightened by a predator or loud noise. It's best if you do not allow children to "play" with the chicks, but it is a good idea to gently place your hand in the brooder so the chicks can get used to you. Once they have accepted your hand in the brooder, you may want to gently stroke them. You'll see that the chicks will soon come running when they see your hand in the brooder. At that point, you can start picking up the chicks and carefully holding them. There is something special about cradling new life in your hands!

When observing your chicks, check them for crooked toes and splayed legs that can cause problems if not treated. Also watch and listen for how your chicks breathe. If you hear that a chick is panting and wheezing, it can mean it is having respiratory issues due to being too hot or that the ammonia levels in the brooder are too high. High ammonia levels are caused by unclean litter from chicken droppings. As you can see, many health issues can be avoided by keeping the litter dry and clean.

It is not necessary to keep the mama hen with her chicks, but if you do have access to her and have not purchased your chicks from a feed store, farmer, or hatchery, she can remain with her chicks to do what all good mammas do—teach them what they need to know to live a happy healthy life…but by the time they reach about six weeks old, the chicks are on their own. Having raised her chicks to this point, the hen starts to lay eggs again. A hen that loves to go broody may try to go broody again as soon as her chicks are on their own.

What's wrong with my Chick?

Even when you are diligent in taking good care of your chicks, there are some ailments and diseases that are common for chicks, and chicks can get sick. Knowing what symptoms to look for or what symptoms are related to a particular disease can give you a starting point for treating your sick chicks. At the very least, you can speak "chicken" with the vet if your chicks get sick and you know about these common ailments.

Pasting Up

When a chick's bottom becomes crusted with poop, it is known as pasting up. Pasting up is very serious and can cause death if not dealt with immediately. As soon as you notice any crust around the chick's bottom, use a warm, wet cloth to hold on the area to loosen the poop and then gently rub it off. This is a tender area and you can harm the chick if you do not wash it very gently. To help soothe the irritated area, rub a tiny bit of coconut oil on it.

Coccidiosis (coc-ci-di-o-sis)

When chicks are kept in soiled litter or damp conditions, the protozoa that are in the intestines of the chicks multiply quickly and they develop coccidiosis. Chicks are susceptible to this.

Picking

Chickens are odd birds, and some of their oddities develop when they are chicks. Sometimes chicks will habitually and almost constantly peck at each other's toes and feathers. Picking seems to start when chicks are in an overcrowded brooder. Not having enough food or not having enough protein in the food, breathing in only stale air, and being overheated also seem to contribute to picking.

Picking can result in the death of chicks. Prevention is the best approach, but if picking starts, the best thing to do is clean the peck wounds on the injured chicks and cover it with healing salve.

It's not difficult to hatch and raise a flock of chicks. Nature takes over and does most of the work for you. Enjoy your chicks while they are chicks because they won't stay small and fuzzy for long!

Kathy Libby Fotolia

Section 6: Keep Your Hens Healthy

For the most part, if you take preventive measures and keep your
henhouse and nesting boxes clean and dry, provide an appropriate
amount of exercise space and level of temperature control, protect your
flock from predators and stressors, and give a balanced diet and plenty of
water, you'll have a healthy flock *most* of the time. But inevitably, one or
more of your chickens will become sick or injured. When this happens,
you will have to make the decision whether you will call a vet that deals
in livestock or try to nurse the chicken back to health yourself. Some
chicken owners feel confident in taking on the role of caring for sick

chickens; others do not. Some argue that a trip to the vet is expensive and if you can't help a chicken with known treatments for a particular set of symptoms, the vet probably can't do much for them either. Only you can choose whether you feel having a vet for your chickens is the best option. If so, you should choose a local vet that treats chickens when you get your flock and let them know that you will bring your chickens in for care and treatment as needed. Doing this ahead of time and keeping the vets' phone number handy can save you precious minutes when a chicken becomes sick.

If you choose not to use a vet for your chickens, another option is to talk with well-established, knowledgeable chicken owners and develop the type of relationships that would permit you to call them if your chickens have health issues. Many are more than happy to help out. You can also read and study about poultry so that you are prepared for emergencies or sudden illness. It is beyond the scope of this guide to provide complete medical and health care information for chickens, but you can learn what to look for and how to treat some of the most common health issues for chickens.

Throughout this guide, you have learned how to help prevent illness and how to quarantine new chickens before allowing them to join your established flock. You also know that when chickens become stressed due to change, being frightened by predators, or have stressors such as not enough food or poor living conditions, they usually succumb to sudden disease and often die. Below is a list of some of the common diseases that plague chickens.

Fowl Pox is a viral disease that can be spread by mosquitoes. Fowl pox can affect chickens of all ages, and can quickly spread through the entire flock once one chicken is infected. Symptoms include wart-like nodules on the skin and in the mouth. Fowl pox is looked upon as the poultry version of chicken pox. Unless it gets in the chicken's respiratory system and impairs breathing, it is usually not fatal, but can last for three to five weeks.

Campylobacteriosis (kam-pi-lo-bak-ter-o-sis) is an infection that is caused by the Campylobacter bacterium. Symptoms include bloody or mucous stools/diarrhea and a shriveled comb. The disease is often brought into the henhouse from an outside source. It can be treated with antibiotics if caught early, but it can cause death.

Avian Influenza is a disease that breeds in the respiratory and intestinal tracks of chickens and other fowl and is transmitted from one bird to another. Symptoms include difficulty breathing and sudden death. The best prevention is vaccination and to cover the chicken run to keep wild birds away from the flock during an outbreak of the virus.

Aspergillosis (as-per-gil-lo-sis) is caused by a fungus-like organism that grows on material such as bedding, rotting wood, old burlap feed sacks, moldy feed, or other decomposing matter. If chickens inhale a large volume of the spores, they can become infected. Again, keeping mold out of the chicken run and henhouse is crucial for healthy chickens.

Bumblefoot is a large growth on the underside of a chickens' foot. It is caused by the infection of a cut or scrape. The bacteria causing the infection may be E. coli or Staphylococcus aureus, which also make people sick so wear disposable gloves when you check your chickens' feet for Bumblefoot. If you suspect that your chicken has Bumblefoot, you can treat it by washing the foot and leg and draining the abscess. Wash the leg and foot with hydrogen peroxide and use an antibiotic ointment. Bandage the foot and leg and keep it bandaged until the foot is healed. Change the dressing at least once every day.

Marek's Disease (mer-iks) is a disease that can cause chickens to not grow and become paralyzed. One of the notable symptoms of this disease is that the chicken will be unnaturally hungry. Marek's Disease can be prevented by vaccinating the newborn chick at a day-old. Marek's Disease is a good reason to never mix new chicks with old chickens.

Fowl Typhoid is a highly infectious and contagious bacterial disease caused by the bacteria *Salmonella Gallinari um*. Chickens of all ages can get the disease, but it occurs more often in younger chickens. The symptoms of the disease are lethargy, no appetite, excessive thirst, yellow or green diarrhea.

Newcastle Disease is a disease that is noted by the chickens' twisted neck, floppy and unsteady stance, and breathing difficulty. Newcastle Disease can be prevented by vaccination. If diagnosed, the chickens with the disease should be separated from the others and slaughtered to keep it from being spread.

Chickens can be bothered by **fleas, lice, and different kinds of mites** such as the Northern fowl mite and red mite. If you notice your chickens scratching, particularly so much so that they create bare patches of skin, check them for fleas, lice, and mites. Tiny mites can burrow under the scales on the legs and cause *scaly leg*. In such a case, the legs look crusty and fat and may remain so until after the chicken goes through the next molting period. You can stick the chicken's leg in a jar of rubbing alcohol for about 20 seconds once a week for a period of about a month to help the chicken heal from scaly leg. Commercial products are also available for scaly leg.

For lice, mites, and such, treat the chickens with commercially prepared flea powder or find a recipe for a natural homemade powder for treatment. Part of getting rid of the fleas or mites includes using flea powder in the henhouse and chicken run, and doing a complete and thorough cleaning of the henhouse.

Your chickens can also develop **parasites and worms,** and if they do, there may not be any outward symptoms. The best thing to do is deworm the chickens every six months with a commercially prepared product.

Did you know that chickens can get **colds**? The best treatment for cold symptoms is probably a commercial blend for colds that you can get from the vet or at the local animal feed store.

Chickens can develop crop bound, particularly if they have been eating long grass. When this happens, the soft crop bulges when the chicken gets up in the morning. The best cure for crop bound is to try to get the chicken to vomit by holding its head back and massaging the crop, and feeding the chicken yogurt with live and active cultures.

Sometimes chickens have **egg binding**, which means they can't pass an egg. The best solution for egg binding is to prevent it by making sure the chicken gets plenty of exercise to help out the process. Sometimes, you have to put on disposable gloves and remove the egg from the vent. Hold the hen firmly under one arm, or ask someone to assist you in holding her, then gently insert your fingers and remove the egg.

Speaking of eggs, if your hen does develop the habit of eating its eggs, it helps to move the nesting box to a darker spot in the henhouse. It's also possible that the chicken is not getting enough calcium in their diet and is eating the egg shell for this reason. This can be remedied by supplying calcium-fortified feed. Calcium is very important for the chickens to produce strong egg shells.

Perhaps the greatest "health" you can give your flock is to be dedicated to their well-being. Sure, things will go wrong as you embark on and travel the path of raising chickens, but your dedication to your flock will see you both through most anything!

In conclusion, this guide is meant to help you raise the healthiest, happiest chickens you can. If you take good care of your flock, observe and learn as much as you can about them, you will be rewarded many times over.

Enjoy the experience!

Made in the USA
Monee, IL
09 July 2021